......ived in Southampton i.. the south of Eng......... everyone was excited about the new ship. It was the biggest ship in the world, the most beautiful, perhaps the fastest. And it was much safer than older ships, because it had sixteen compartments with emergency doors. The new ship had radio too. Passengers could send messages from the ship to their friends at home!

Captain Smith and his officers and sailors were ready. Then the passengers came – millionaires, young people, families of six, people from more than forty different countries. Many of them wanted to begin a new life in America.

So the *Titanic* went to Cherbourg in France, then Queenstown in Ireland, and then left for New York. There were 2,224 people on the ship, but there were lifeboats for only half of them. But that did not matter. The *Titanic* was unsinkable . . .

OXFORD BOOKWORMS LIBRARY

Factfiles

Titanic

Stage 1 (400 headwords)

Factfiles Series Editor: Christine Lindop

TIM VICARY

Titanic

OXFORD UNIVERSITY PRESS

OXFORD
UNIVERSITY PRESS

Great Clarendon Street, Oxford OX2 6DP

Oxford University Press is a department of the University of Oxford.
It furthers the University's objective of excellence in research, scholarship,
and education by publishing worldwide in

Oxford New York

Auckland Cape Town Dar es Salaam Hong Kong Karachi
Kuala Lumpur Madrid Melbourne Mexico City Nairobi
New Delhi Shanghai Taipei Toronto

With offices in

Argentina Austria Brazil Chile Czech Republic France Greece
Guatemala Hungary Italy Japan Poland Portugal Singapore
South Korea Switzerland Thailand Turkey Ukraine Vietnam

OXFORD and OXFORD ENGLISH are registered trade marks of
Oxford University Press in the UK and in certain other countries

ISBN: 978 0 19 423619 5

A complete recording of this Bookworms edition of *Titanic*
is available on audio CD ISBN 978 0 19 423620 1

Printed in Hong Kong

Word count (main text): 5,529

For more information on the Oxford Bookworms Library,
visit www.oup.com/bookworms

ACKNOWLEDGEMENTS

Cover illustration Merie W. Wallace/20th Century Fox/Paramount 1997/film stills from *Titanic*
Illustration pp38–39 by Gareth Riddiford

The publishers would like to thank the following for permission to reproduce images:

Allstar Picture Library pp12 (ship scene from *Titanic* (1997) filmstill/Cinetext/20th Century Fox), 20 (lifeboats from *Titanic* (1997) filmstill/Cinetext/20th Century Fox), 23 (into the lifeboats from *Titanic* (1997) filmstill/Cinetext/20th Century Fox), 40 (*Titanic* (1997) poster/20th Century Fox); Corbis pp1 (*Titanic* shipwreck/Ralph White/Comet), 11 (*Titanic* impact illustration/Bettmann), 18 (SS Carpathia wireless room/Bettmann), 26 (Sinking of the *Titanic* by Willy Stoewer/Bettmann), 30 (*Titanic* Survivors Board *Carpathia*/Bettmann), 32 (rescued passenger/Underwood & Underwood/Bettmann), 33 (newsboy with *Titanic* headline/Hulton-Deutsch Collection); Davison & Associates Ltd p5 (White Star Wharf, Queenstown/Father Browne); Getty Images ppviii (*Titanic* postcard/Popperfoto), 4 (*Titanic* gymnasium/ Popperfoto), 9 (The Marconi Room, *Titanic* /Popperfoto), 10 (iceberg/Dale Wilson/Photographer's Choice), 14 (*Titanic* cross-section/Hulton Archive), 27 (*Titanic* sinking illustration/Dorling Kindersley); Kobal Collection p16 (*Titanic* sinking from *Titanic* (1997) filmstill/20th Century Fox/Paramount/Wallace, Merie W.); Mary Evans Picture Library pp3 (Tea Room/Illustrated London News Ltd), 4 (Mr & Mrs Astor/ Illustrated London News Ltd), 8 (J. Bruce Ismay/Illustrated London News Ltd), 9 (Jack Philips/Illustrated London News Ltd), 25 (*Titanic* musicians/Illustrated London News Ltd), 28 (Fifth Officer Harold Lowe/ Illustrated London News Ltd), 36 (Second Officer Charles Lightoller/Illustrated London News Ltd); Mirrorpix p6 (passenger deck/John Reavenall); National Museums Northern Ireland/Ulster Folk and Transport Museum pp2 (The Great Gantry, Queens Island, Belfast), 7 (Thomas Andrews), 13 (*Titanic* Crew); OUP p44 (iceberg/Corbis/Digital Stock), (lifeboats/Photodisc), (fireworks/Photodisc), (lifejacket/ Photodisc), (stars/Photodisc), (baby/Photodisc); Rex Features p35 (Millvina Dean/Mike Lawn); Straus Historical Society, Inc. p22 (Isidor & Ida Straus).

CONTENTS

The *Titanic, 1912*

1 Under the sea

It was 1 September 1985. Under a ship in the North Atlantic, a camera moved through the dark water. Slowly, the camera went down – 1,000 metres, 2,000 metres, 3,000 metres under the sea. On the ship, some sailors waited and watched. Nobody spoke. Then, suddenly, they saw something.

The *Titanic*, 1985

'There it is!'

'Where?'

'There – look, I can see it!'

'Yes, you're right! It's the *Titanic!*'

With the camera, the sailors could see a ship 3,810 metres under the water. It was a very big, old ship, and it was in two halves. They could see the front half of the ship with their camera, but the back half of the ship was 800 metres away.

The sailors were all very happy. They took

lots of photographs. The next year they came back with more cameras. The cameras went down under the sea and looked at the ship more carefully. They went all round the ship, and took hundreds of photos. Some of the cameras went into the ship too, through the windows. Later there was a film about the ship. People all over the world watched the film, and saw the photographs in newspapers.

But who built the *Titanic*? What happened to it? Why did it break in two halves, and sink to the bottom of the sea? And what about the people on this ship? What were they like, and what happened to them?

This is the story of the *Titanic*.

Building the *Titanic* in Belfast

2 The biggest ship in the world

More than 15,000 people built the *Titanic* in Belfast, Northern Ireland. They began building it in 1909, and finished it in 1912. The *Titanic* was the biggest ship in the world – 46,328 tons, 265 metres long, and 28 metres across. It had three big engines, and it could go at 23 knots (46 kilometres per hour) so it was one of the fastest ships in the world, too.

The *Titanic* was very safe. It had sixteen compartments and fifteen emergency doors. When the captain closed the emergency doors, water could not move from one compartment to the next one. 'The new *Titanic* is much safer than older ships,' a newspaper said.

The *Titanic* was a very beautiful ship. The rooms for the first-class passengers, like Mr and Mrs John Jacob Astor IV, were like rooms in a very expensive hotel. John Jacob Astor was one of the richest men in the

A first-class lounge

world. He was forty-seven years old, but his second wife, Madeleine, was only eighteen. On the ship, Mr and Mrs Astor had two big bedrooms, a sitting room, and three more rooms.

Mr Astor and his young wife could eat in the beautiful restaurant, and talk to rich, famous people, like Benjamin Guggenheim, an American businessman, Colonel Archibald Gracie, a soldier and writer, and Mr Isidor Straus, a businessman from New York, with his wife Ida. The captain of the *Titanic*, Edward Smith, came to eat with them too. There were many more rooms for the first-class passengers; there they could walk, read, smoke, and listen to music.

Mr and Mrs Astor

The first-class gymnasium

Third-class passengers waiting for the *Titanic*

The rooms for the second-class passengers were beautiful too. They were better than the first-class rooms on most ships.

But most of the passengers had third-class tickets. These people were not rich; they were working people from England, Ireland, and many more countries. Carla Jensen was a nineteen-year-old girl from Denmark, and Anna Turja was eighteen and from Finland. These two young women wanted to begin a new life in America.

Third-class passengers had small rooms called cabins on E deck, a long way under the first-class and second-class passengers. There were four beds in every cabin. Sometimes the first-class passengers walked their dogs on E deck, because it had the longest corridors on the ship. But they did not talk to the third-class passengers. They had nothing to say to them.

3   A city on the sea

On 10 April 1912, the *Titanic* left Southampton in the south of England. The ship went to Cherbourg in France, and then to Queenstown, near the city of Cork in Ireland. A lot of third-class passengers got on here. Then the *Titanic* went west towards New York.

On Sunday 14 April Colonel Gracie got up early. He had breakfast, finished reading a book, and talked to his friends Mr and Mrs Straus.

On the boat deck, Mrs Astor talked to Thomas Andrews, the designer of the *Titanic*. 'I know all about this ship,' he said. 'Do you have any questions, Mrs Astor?'

'Yes,' she said. 'How many people are there on this ship?'

The boat deck

Thomas Andrews took a book out of his pocket. 'Let me see . . . there are 325 first-class passengers, like us; 277 second-class passengers; 706 third-class passengers; 908 officers and sailors – and 8 musicians.'

'My goodness! We're like a small city, aren't we?' Mrs Astor put her hand on a small boat on the side of the ship. 'How many of these lifeboats are there?'

'Twenty.'

'Twenty?' Mrs Astor said. 'But . . . can all those people get into twenty lifeboats?'

'No, of course not,' Thomas Andrews said quietly. 'But don't be afraid, Mrs Astor. We don't really need the lifeboats, because the *Titanic* can never sink. It is the safest ship in the world.'

The President of the White Star Line, J. Bruce Ismay, was excited about his new ship. He talked to Captain Smith. 'How fast can the *Titanic* go?' Bruce Ismay asked.

'About 23 knots,' Captain Smith answered. 'But we're

Thomas Andrews

going about 18 knots now. We don't want to arrive in New York a day early, do we?'

'Why not?' Bruce Ismay laughed. 'Come on, Captain, let's get there early. The *Titanic* is going to be famous!'

Down on E deck, the third-class passengers talked about America, in many languages. Carla Jensen was Danish, but there were two English girls and a Swedish girl in her cabin. Carla's brother Svend and her father's brother Niels were on the *Titanic* too. In Anna Turja's cabin there were two young Finnish women and some children.

Millvina Dean was the youngest passenger on the *Titanic*. She was a baby, only nine weeks old. Sidney Goodwin was two years old. He had a big family – his mother and father, two sisters and three brothers were all in the same cabin.

Many passengers sent radio messages. In 1912, radio was very new. The two radio operators, Jack Phillips and

J. Bruce Ismay

The *Titanic's* radio room

Jack Phillips

Harold Bride, had a lot of work. In three days they sent 250 messages, and more messages came in – from New York, from Southampton, and from ships.

A lot of the radio messages from ships talked about ice. 'Be careful, there are a lot of icebergs in the North Atlantic,' the messages said. But Captain Smith was not very worried. He only showed one of these messages to his officers.

The *Titanic* did not go slower because of the ice. It went on across the Atlantic, at more than 20 knots. The passengers walked round the ship; they laughed and talked and ate in the restaurants. Everyone was happy and excited. The lights were on, and the music played. Mrs Astor was right. The *Titanic* was like a small city, far away on a big, cold sea.

4 Iceberg!

On the night of 14 April, the weather was good and there were lots of stars in the night sky. The sea was quiet, but it was very cold.

High up in the ship, two sailors – Frederick Fleet and Reginald Lee – looked out at the black sea and sky. The two men were very cold. At 11.40 p.m. Fleet saw something in front of the ship. It was very big and white, and it was not far away.

'Iceberg! Iceberg!' he said on the telephone. 'There's an iceberg in front of the ship!'

An iceberg

'Thank you,' First Officer Murdoch answered. 'Turn left, quickly,' he told Robert Hitchens, the sailor next to him. But big ships turn much more slowly than smaller ones. And the *Titanic* was the biggest ship in the world.

For 37 long seconds, nothing happened. The *Titanic* went towards the iceberg – a million tons of ice – at 40 kilometres per hour. Then, very slowly, the ship began to turn left. Fleet and Lee watched, their mouths open. The iceberg came nearer and nearer. They heard the noise when it hit the right side of the ship. They could see ice down on the deck. Then the iceberg went behind the ship, away into the black night.

First Officer Murdoch's face was white. 'Stop the engines, quickly,' he said. The engines stopped, and the *Titanic* moved slower and slower. Then it stopped.

Many passengers were asleep, and did not hear anything. But Colonel Gracie did. He looked at his watch; it was 11.45 p.m. He

The *Titanic* hits the iceberg: a passenger's drawing

The *Titanic* moved slower, then it stopped

opened his cabin door and looked out. It was very quiet.
'Why can't I hear the engines?' he thought. He put on a
warm coat and went out onto the deck.

Some passengers saw the ice on the deck and laughed.
'Let's put it in our drinks!' they said. They played with the
ice for a few minutes and then went in, out of the cold.

But down in the third-class cabins at the front of the
ship, the iceberg made much more noise when it hit the
ship. Water came into Daniel Buckley's cabin. He got
up and opened his door. There were a lot of people in
the corridor. 'What's happening?' they asked. 'What's
wrong?'

The four girls in Carla Jensen's cabin woke up, but then
they went back to sleep. Carla was in bed in her nightdress
when Niels Jensen opened the door at 12.30 a.m. 'Come
on, Carla, get up,' he said. 'Something's happening.
We must go up on deck.' So Carla put a coat over her
nightdress, and went upstairs with Niels. She never saw
the girls in her cabin again.

A man opened Anna Turja's cabin door too. 'Put on
your life jackets, girls, quickly!' he said. 'We're all going
into the sea!'

5 CQD – emergency!

Captain Smith heard the noise too. He got out of bed quickly. 'What's wrong?' he asked First Officer Murdoch. 'What was that noise?'

'An iceberg, sir,' Murdoch answered. 'I'm very sorry, but we hit an iceberg. I'm stopping the engines.'

Slowly, the *Titanic* stopped. The big, beautiful ship waited on the quiet black sea, under a thousand stars.

'Close the emergency doors, quickly!' said Captain Smith.

'They are closed, sir.'

'That's good. Well done.'

When the fifteen emergency doors were closed, water

White Star Line officers, with Captain Smith (front centre right) and First Officer Murdoch (front right)

could not move along the ship, from one compartment into the next one. But how many holes were there in the ship? Was there just one hole in one compartment, or were there a lot of holes, in a lot of compartments? Captain Smith wanted to know the answer – quickly.

Inside the *Titanic*

Captain Smith, First Officer Murdoch, and Thomas Andrews, the designer of the *Titanic,* went down into the ship. They found a lot of holes. There was water in compartments 1, 2, 3, 4, and 5. 'How bad is this?' Captain Smith asked.

Thomas Andrews' face was white; he looked very unhappy. 'Very bad, I'm afraid,' he answered. 'This ship is going to sink.'

'What do you mean?' Captain Smith said. 'The *Titanic* can't sink. You said that to Mrs Astor yesterday! I heard you!'

'Yes, I know,' Andrews said. 'The *Titanic* is safe with water in three compartments. In fact, it is nearly safe with water in four compartments. But this – this is different. The water is coming into *five* compartments. *Five.* The front of the ship is going to get heavier and heavier – I'm sorry, but we can't stop it. The *Titanic* is going to sink.'

'How long have we got?' Captain Smith asked.

'I don't know. Two hours, perhaps. That's all.'

'Right. Give the passengers their life jackets, and get the lifeboats ready,' Smith said to Murdoch. Then he walked into the radio room to speak to the *Titanic*'s radio operator, Jack Phillips.

'This is an emergency,' Captain Smith said. 'The ship is sinking. Ask for help.'

'Yes, sir,' Jack Phillips answered. He sent the emergency message. 'CQD – MGY. (Help – *Titanic*). We are sinking. Please come to help us.' It was 12.15 a.m.

6   Nobody is listening

The nearest ship to the *Titanic* was the *Californian*. It was about 16 kilometres away. The *Californian* knew about the ice, so it stopped at 10.30 that night. At 11.10 the third officer, Charles Groves, saw the lights of a big ship on the right. The *Californian* tried to send a message with a light to the ship, but there was no answer. At 11.40, the big ship stopped, but Charles Groves did not know why. He did not know that it was the *Titanic*.

In 1912, radio was very new. Most ships had radio, but they didn't listen to it all the time. Cyril Evans, the radio

Rockets from the *Titanic*

operator on the *Californian*, went to bed at 11.30. So nobody on the *Californian* heard the emergency message from Jack Phillips at 12.15 a.m.

People at Cape Race in America heard it, and one man heard it in New York. But for nearly ten minutes, no ships answered the message.

Then, at 12.25, the radio operator on a ship called *Carpathia* wanted to talk to the *Titanic*. '*Titanic*, I have a message for one of your passengers,' he said. 'Are you listening?'

'Come at once,' Jack Phillips answered. 'This is an emergency. We need help. We are sinking.'

'Shall I tell the captain?' the *Carpathia*'s radio operator asked.

'Yes please, quickly!' Phillips answered. So at 12.35 the

Carpathia began to go towards the *Titanic*. But the *Carpathia* was 92 kilometres away.

From the *Titanic*, Captain Smith could see the *Californian*, but he did not know its name, and he could not talk to it on the radio. Jack Phillips tried to call it with the letters CQD and SOS, but nothing happened. Captain Smith tried to send a message with a light, but it did not answer. 'It's no good,' he said. 'Send up the rockets.'

At 12.45 the first rocket went

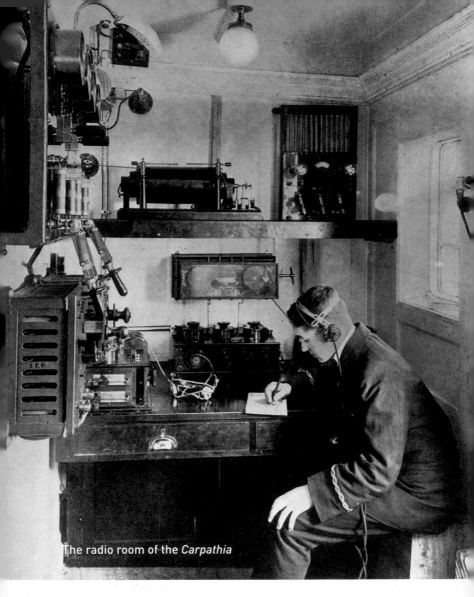

The radio room of the *Carpathia*

up into the night sky. It made white lights high over the *Titanic*. Every ten minutes after that, a new rocket went up. On the *Californian*, Second Officer Stone saw the rockets. 'That's interesting,' he said. He told his captain, Captain Lord. But Captain Lord was tired, so he went to bed. Stone watched the rockets for over an hour. But he did not understand them, so he did nothing.

7 Into the lifeboats

The *Titanic* had twenty lifeboats. These boats could carry 1,178 people, but there were 2,224 people on the ship. So for nearly half of the people on the ship, there was no lifeboat.

The first boat, Lifeboat 7, went into the sea at 12.55 a.m. with twenty-six people. Lifeboat 1 could take sixty people, but there were only twelve people in it. Lifeboat 6 had only twenty-five women and one sailor.

The ship's officers helped the passengers with their life jackets. 'Women and children must go in the lifeboats,' the officers said. 'Men must stay on the ship.' But some of the women did not want to go. It was warm on the ship, and cold in the dark sea.

Young Mrs Astor was cold. She wore a life jacket over her beautiful blue dress, but she did not have a warm coat. She wanted to stay on the ship with her husband. 'I don't need to go in a lifeboat,' she said. 'The *Titanic* can't sink. Thomas Andrews told me that.' Mr Astor sat on a chair next to his wife. 'Let's stay on the ship,' he said. 'We're safer here than in that little boat.'

For half an hour Mrs Astor sat with her husband. They watched women and children get into the lifeboats. They saw the sea come nearer and nearer. 'It's no good,' she said at last. 'Mr Andrews was wrong. This ship *is* sinking.' Second Officer Charles Lightoller helped Mrs

Astor into Lifeboat 4. Mr Astor wanted to go with her. 'Can't I go with my wife?' he said, 'She needs me – she's going to have a baby.'

'I'm sorry, sir,' Charles Lightoller said. 'These boats are for women and children. Men must stay here.'

Mr Astor watched his wife go down into the sea in the lifeboat. 'Don't be afraid,' he said. 'I'm going to be OK. We can meet in New York.'

'Goodbye, my love,' she said. She never saw him again.

Isidor Straus was sixty-seven years old, and his wife was sixty-three. 'I'm not going without my husband,' Mrs Straus said. 'Where he goes, I go.'

'That's OK,' said Charles Lightoller. 'He's an old man, so he can go with the women.'

'No,' said Mr Straus. 'I'm a man. I'm staying here, with the men.' So Mrs Straus stayed with her husband on the *Titanic*.

The lifeboats were on the boat deck, near the first-class and second-class passengers. Anna Turja ran upstairs from E deck towards the boat deck.

'Stop!' a sailor said. 'You can't go up there!' Anna did not stop, but the sailor closed the door behind her. There were hundreds of angry passengers on E deck, behind the closed doors. 'Let us out!' they said. 'We're all going to die!' Then Daniel Buckley and some more men broke the door, and ran up the stairs.

A lot of men were afraid, and angry. 'We must get on a boat!' they said. But the officers on the boat deck had guns. 'Stand back!' they said. 'Women and children only!'

Mr and Mrs Straus

But Daniel Buckley got into a boat and put on a woman's hat. When the officers looked into that boat, they saw only women there. Some third-class women passengers, like Anna Turja and Carla Jensen, got into the boats too. Carla was cold. She had no shoes – just a nightdress, a life jacket, and a coat.

Eighteen of the *Titanic*'s twenty lifeboats went into the sea. Some had only ten or twenty people in them, but Lifeboat 14 had Fifth Officer Lowe with fifty-eight women and children. After that there were only two lifeboats, Lifeboats A and B, on the ship.

'Women and children only!'

8 In the cold, dark sea

The eight musicians did not get into the lifeboats. They stayed on the *Titanic* and played music – happy music, for worried people.

Benjamin Guggenheim, the rich businessman, and his friend watched the women get into the lifeboats. They stood quietly and listened to the music. Then they took off their life jackets and put on their best coats. 'Now we are ready to die,' they said.

'Help the passengers,' Captain Smith said to the sailors. 'The ship is going down. You can do no more.' Thomas Andrews, the designer of the *Titanic*, said nothing. What could he say?

Second Officer Lightoller and Colonel Gracie wanted to move Lifeboats A and B, but it was not easy. Water came back along the ship, faster and faster. Lifeboat A went into the sea. There was nobody in it at first, but then some men got in. Lifeboat B went into the sea the wrong way up.

Suddenly the ship moved, and Colonel Gracie and Charles Lightoller fell into the ice cold sea. They went a long way under the water. 'I'm going to die,' Colonel Gracie thought.

Then at last they came up, and swam to Lifeboat B. But Lifeboat B was the wrong way up. They could not get *into* it, so they got *onto* it. Radio Operator Jack Phillips

Musicians of the *Titanic*

was on top of Lifeboat B, with Colonel Gracie, Charles Lightoller, and twenty-six more men. Radio Operator Harold Bride was *under* Lifeboat B at first. Then he swam out and got on top.

'That's good, boys,' said an old man in the water near Lifeboat B. 'You're going to be OK.' But he did not get onto the boat, and after some time, he died. 'Who was that?' the men asked. 'Captain Smith, perhaps?'

The front of the ship went down, and at the same time the back of the ship went up. For two minutes the back of the ship went slowly up, higher and higher. Some people ran to the back of the ship; a lot of people fell from the ship into the sea.

Carla Jensen watched from Lifeboat 16. 'The sea was

very quiet and dark,' she said later. 'The lights were still on in the ship. Then, suddenly, there was a terrible noise. A thousand people cried from the ship – we heard them. Then the *Titanic* broke into two halves.'

Slowly at first, then faster and faster, the *Titanic* went under the water. First the front of the ship went under, then the back. At 2.20 a.m. the *Titanic* was not there. The people in the boats could see the stars in the night sky, and the black sea, but no *Titanic*. The biggest ship in the world was under the sea.

There were more than a thousand people in the water. Most of them had life jackets, so their heads stayed out of the water. But the sea water was very cold, and nobody could live in it for long. 'Please, come back and help us!' the people in the water cried to the people in the lifeboats.

In Lifeboat 6 there was one sailor and twenty-five

women. 'We must go back to help the people in the water,' some of the women said. 'Our husbands are there – they need help!' 'No,' said the sailor, Robert Hitchens. 'There are too many people in the water. They can't all get in this boat – it isn't safe!'

So they did nothing. Lifeboat 1 had only twelve people in it, but they did not take one man or woman out of the sea.

But in Lifeboat 14, Fifth Officer Lowe did want to help. 'Get into Lifeboats 10 and 12,' he told his fifty-eight passengers. 'Quickly, now. This boat is going back.' But it was not easy to move the passengers. Then, at 3.00 a.m. Fifth Officer Lowe went back with Lifeboat 14 to help the people in the water. But it was too late. Nearly everyone was dead. Harold Lowe took only four people alive out of the sea.

They saw one man on a

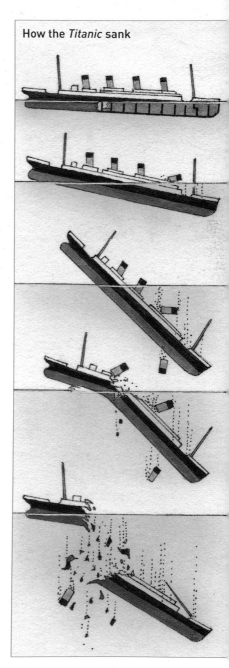

How the *Titanic* sank

Fifth Officer Harold Lowe

door in the water. He looked cold and white and dead.
But after a few minutes he opened his eyes, and began to
talk – in Japanese! Later, he helped to row the boat, like a
sailor. 'What a good man!' Harold Lowe said.

All night, people sat in the lifeboats, and waited for
morning. When the sun came up, they looked at the cold,
quiet sea. They could see icebergs everywhere. And in the
water, near the icebergs, they saw hundreds of cold, white
bodies – the bodies of dead passengers and sailors.

9   The *Carpathia* and the *Californian*

The *Carpathia* heard the message from the *Titanic* at 12.25 a.m. It came very quickly – at 15 knots (31 kilometres per hour) – towards the *Titanic*. At 2.35 Captain Rostron, the captain of the *Carpathia*, saw a green light over the sea. At 2.45 his sailors saw an iceberg. Then more icebergs. 'We're going very fast, sir, it isn't safe,' a sailor said. 'Don't stop,' said Captain Rostron. 'We must get there quickly. The *Titanic* is sinking.'

There were no more radio messages from the *Titanic*. At 4.00 a.m. the *Carpathia* stopped, and sent some rockets into the air. 'Here we are,' the captain said. 'But where is the *Titanic*?'

The sun came up. There was no *Titanic*. They saw more than twenty icebergs, some big, some small. And one small lifeboat, 400 metres away. There was a sailor in it, some women, and a baby.

'Where is the *Titanic*?' Captain Rostron asked.

'It went down, sir,' answered the sailor. 'An hour and a half ago.'

On the *Californian*, Chief Officer Stewart saw the *Carpathia*. 'There's that ship,' he said to Captain Lord. 'It's firing rockets again.'

'It doesn't matter,' said Captain Lord. 'It's not important.'

Taking a lifeboat onto the *Carpathia*

But at 5.40 a.m. Evans, the radio operator on the *Californian*, got out of bed. 'Speak to that ship, Evans, please,' Stewart said. 'Why are they firing rockets?'

Two minutes later, Evans answered, 'That ship is the *Carpathia*, sir. There are lifeboats in the sea and the *Carpathia* is helping them. The *Titanic* hit an iceberg last night.'

'We must help, too,' said Captain Lord. 'Quickly!' So the *Californian* went towards the *Carpathia*. But it was nearly 6.00 a.m. – more than five long hours after the *Titanic* needed their help.

Slowly, more lifeboats came to the *Carpathia*. Lifeboat B began to sink, and the people on the boat climbed onto Lifeboat 12. At 8.30 a.m. Lifeboat 12 arrived at the *Carpathia* with seventy-five people in it. There was a lot of water in the boat, and all the passengers were tired and cold. It was the last of the lifeboats from the *Titanic*. Second Officer Lightoller helped people onto the ship, and then he got out of the lifeboat and onto the ship too. He was the last person from the *Titanic* to come onto the *Carpathia*.

The sailors from the *Carpathia* helped the passengers onto their ship. They had warm coats and hot drinks for them. But the passengers wanted to know about their families and friends. 'Is my husband here?' they asked. 'Is my wife here? Where are my children?'

Four days later the *Carpathia* arrived in New York with 711 people from the *Titanic*. But back in the cold North Atlantic, 1,513 people were dead. An important man, Senator Smith, began to ask questions. 'What went

Titanic passengers on the *Carpathia*

wrong?' he wanted to know. 'Why did the *Titanic* sink? Why did all these people die?'

Captain Smith and First Officer Murdoch were dead, and the designer Thomas Andrews was dead too. But the President of the White Star Line, Bruce Ismay, was on the *Carpathia*, so Senator Smith talked to him.

'Did you know about the icebergs?' Senator Smith asked.

'Well, Captain Smith knew about them, yes,' Bruce Ismay answered.

'Then why didn't the *Titanic* go slower?' Senator Smith asked. 'Did you talk to Captain Smith about that?'

'Me? No, of course not,' Bruce Ismay answered. 'He was the captain, I was only a passenger.'

'A passenger, yes – but you were the President of the White Star Line too,' Senator Smith said angrily. 'The

Titanic was your ship, and 1,500 people died because the *Titanic* hit an iceberg. Can you answer *this* question, then? Why did you only have twenty lifeboats?'

Bruce Ismay looked unhappy. 'Because the *Titanic* could not sink! Thomas Andrews told me that. He was the designer – he knew about ships. And remember, it had sixteen compartments and fifteen emergency doors. "We don't need a lot of lifeboats – it's the safest ship in the world," Andrews said. And I listened to him.'

'I see,' Senator Smith said angrily. 'So *you* did nothing wrong. Captain Smith was wrong about the icebergs, and Thomas Andrews was wrong about the lifeboats. But *you*, the President of the White Star Line . . .'

'I was only a passenger,' Bruce Ismay said.

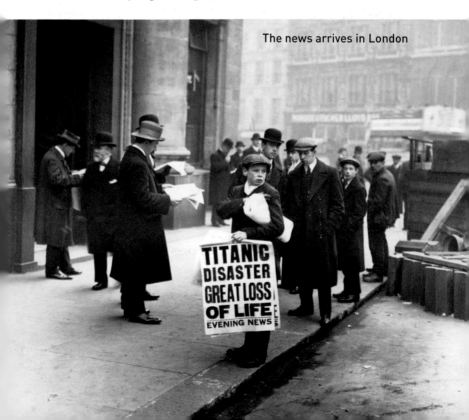

The news arrives in London

10 Life after the *Titanic*

What happened to the people from the *Titanic*?

The American ship *Mackay-Bennett* found hundreds of dead bodies in the sea. One of the bodies was John Jacob Astor. He was buried in New York in May 1912. In August 1912, Mrs Astor had a baby son. She called him John Jacob Astor, the same name as his father. Mrs Astor died in 1953.

The *Mackay-Bennett* also found Mr Straus, and he was buried in New York, too. But they did not find his wife.

Many of the bodies on the *Mackay-Bennett* had no names. One of the bodies was a baby, two years old. Nobody knew his name then, so they called him 'the unknown child'. Today, we know that he was Sidney Goodwin. His mother and father, three brothers and two sisters all died in the sea too. Little Sidney, like many of the *Titanic* passengers, was buried in Halifax, Nova Scotia, in Canada.

But Millvina Dean, the youngest passenger on the *Titanic,* did not die. She left the *Titanic* in Lifeboat 10 with her mother and brother. Later they returned to England on another White Star ship, the *Adriatic*. All the women passengers on the *Adriatic* wanted to hold her in their arms. In the end, one of the officers said, 'No passenger can hold Millvina for more than ten minutes.'

Colonel Archibald Gracie wrote a book about the

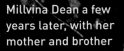

Titanic, but he never really got well after his time in the sea. He died in December 1912, and his last words were, 'We must get them all in the boats.'

It was not easy for Anna Turja in America. She did not know any people there, and she could not speak English. A hospital doctor in New York wrote her name on her arm, and put her on a train to her brother in Ohio.

But Anna was a beautiful, friendly young woman. She met her husband in Ohio, and they had seven children. She died in 1982, aged eighty-nine.

Carla Jensen went back to Denmark. She met her husband, and they had three children. She died on 14 March 1980, and she was buried in her old nightdress from the *Titanic*.

Second Officer
Charles Lightoller

Daniel Buckley went to France in 1914 to be a soldier. He died in 1918. Jack Phillips died from cold in the lifeboat. His friend Harold Bride, the second radio operator, went home to Scotland. He met his wife there, and they had three children. He died in 1956, aged sixty-six. Fifth Officer Harold Lowe died in May 1944, in Wales.

Second Officer Charles Lightoller had an exciting life. After the *Titanic*, he worked on a White Star ship called the *Oceanic*; but in 1914, the *Oceanic* sank too. Then he worked on a ship called the *Falcon*, but the *Falcon* also sank. In 1940, at the age of sixty-six, he went with his son Roger in his small boat called *Sundowner* to Dunkirk in France. *Sundowner* was not much bigger than one of the *Titanic*'s lifeboats, but it carried 130 soldiers home across the sea to England. Charles Lightoller died in 1952, in London, aged seventy-eight.

Bruce Ismay went home to England, and the White Star Line finished their new ship – the *Britannic*. But Ismay's later life was not happy. He could never forget the *Titanic*.

11 Finding the *Titanic*

There are many stories about the *Titanic*. A man called Walter Lord talked to hundreds of passengers and sailors and in 1956 he wrote about them in his book, *A Night to Remember*. In 1957 there was a film of the book called *A Night to Remember*. Anna Turja went to see the film, but she could not speak English. So her son watched the film with her and told her about it.

But Anna did not really understand about films. 'Those people with the film cameras,' she said to her son when they came out of the cinema. 'They made this film when the *Titanic* went down. So why didn't they help all the people in the water?'

In 1985 Robert Ballard went to look for the *Titanic*, first on a French ship, and then on an American ship. He found the *Titanic* 3,810 metres under the sea, 531 kilometres south-east of Newfoundland. In 1986 and 1987 he went back with more cameras and made a film about the ship under the sea.

In 1987 James Cameron saw this film and said: 'I must make a Hollywood film about this.' In 1995 he went to see the *Titanic* under the sea, and he got money to make his film. Cameron's film, *Titanic*, was very expensive; he needed 200 million dollars for it. That is 1 million dollars for every minute of the film. In the film, Kate Winslet, a rich girl, meets Leonardo DiCaprio, a poor boy. When the

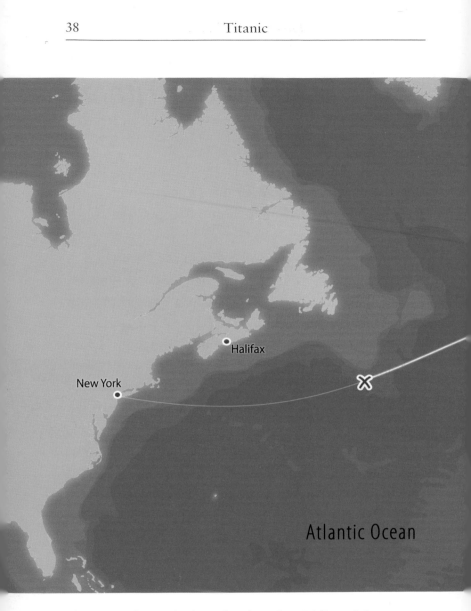

Halifax

New York

Atlantic Ocean

ship goes down the boy dies but the girl lives. Many years later, the girl is an old lady. She goes back to look at the ship under the sea, and tells her story.

Not everything in the film is true, but most of it is. By 1997 most of the passengers from the *Titanic* were dead.

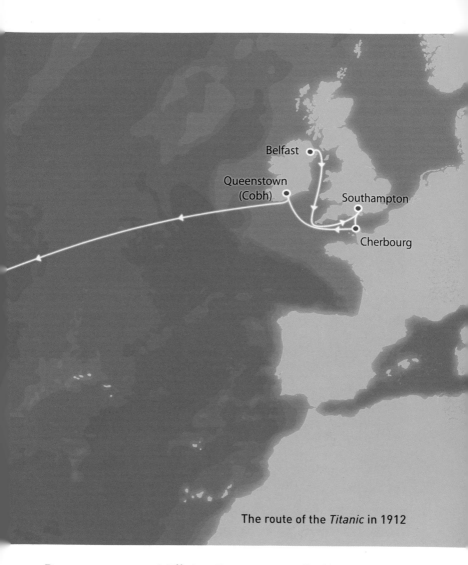

The route of the *Titanic* in 1912

But one woman, Millvina Dean, was still alive. In 1912, she was the youngest passenger on the *Titanic*, but in 1997 she was an old lady. She went across the Atlantic again, on a big fast ship, the *QE2*. Millvina Dean looked out at the sea and the icebergs, and thought about the *Titanic*.

FROM THE DIRECTOR OF 'ALIENS,' 'T2' AND 'TRUE LIES'

LEONARDO DiCAPRIO · KATE WINSLET

TITANIC

'I was here, eighty-five years ago,' she said. 'We were on the biggest, most beautiful ship in the world. But I was a little baby then, in my mother's arms. So I can't really remember anything of that night, on 14 April 1912.'

In 2008 Millvina Dean was the only passenger alive from the *Titanic*. But people still talk and think and write about the *Titanic*. They remember it because it was big, and fast, and beautiful, of course. But they also remember the cold night in 1912 when the 'safest ship in the world' went to the bottom of the sea.

GLOSSARY

baby a very young child

boat a small ship for travelling on water

bottom the lowest part of something

bury to put a dead body in the ground

captain the person who is in charge of a ship

city a large town

compartment a separate part of a room or building, like a large box

corridor a long narrow passage inside a building, with rooms on each side

deck one of the floors of a ship

designer the person who makes the plans that show how to make something

emergency a sudden dangerous situation, when people need help quickly

engine a machine that makes things move

fall to go quickly from a higher place to a lower place

film a story in pictures that you see at the cinema

gun a thing that shoots out bullets to kill people

ice water that has become hard because it has frozen; **iceberg** a very big piece of ice in the sea

life the time that you are alive

lifeboat a small boat on a ship that people can use if the ship is sinking

life jacket something you wear to help you stay alive in the water

light something that gives light to help you see, or to get attention

message words that one person sends to another

music when you sing or play an instrument, you make music; **musician** a person who makes music

officer a person on a ship who is in charge of other people

operator a person who makes a machine work

passenger   a person who is travelling on a ship but not working
  on it
president   the person with the highest position in a company
restaurant   a place where people can buy and eat meals
rocket   a bright light that goes up into the sky
safe   not in danger
sailor   a person who works on a ship
send   to make something go somewhere, especially a letter or a
  message
side   the part of something that is not the top, bottom, front or
  back
sink   to go down under water
small   little
soldier   a person in an army
star   one of the small bright lights that you see in the sky at night
story   words that tell you about what happened in a certain place
  or time
terrible   very bad
towards   in the direction of something
world   the Earth with all its countries and people
worried   afraid and unhappy because you think something bad is
  going to happen

The *Titanic*

ACTIVITIES

ACTIVITIES

Before Reading

1 **Match the words to the pictures. You can use a dictionary.**

1 ☐ life jacket   2 ☐ baby   3 ☐ stars
4 ☐ iceberg   5 ☐ rockets   6 ☐ lifeboats

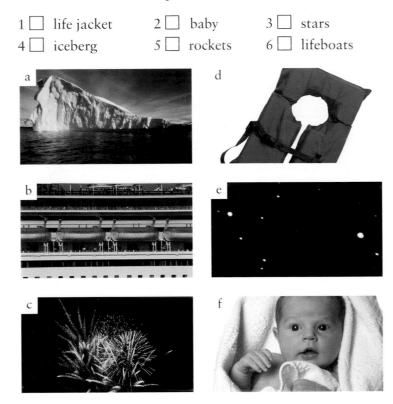

2 **All the words in question 1 are used in the story of the**
Titanic. Can you guess why they are in the story? Make
sentences about the _Titanic_ using these words.

ACTIVITIES

While Reading

Read Chapter 1. Choose the right words to complete these sentences.

bottom, cameras, carefully, film, halves, newspapers, photographs, sailors

1 The *Titanic* was in two _____ at the _____ of the sea.
2 The _____ were happy because they could take lots of

   _____.

3 A year later, the sailors came back with more _____
   and looked at the ship more _____.
4 People all over the world watched a _____ about the
   ship, and saw photographs in the _____.

Read Chapter 2. Are these sentences true (T) or false (F)? Change the false sentences into true ones.

1 Thousands of people built the *Titanic* in London.
2 The *Titanic* was the biggest ship in the world.
3 John Jacob Astor was a very rich man.
4 Astor's wife Madeleine was thirty-eight years old.
5 Edward Smith was the designer of the *Titanic*.
6 Most of the passengers were rich people.
7 Carla Jensen was a third-class passenger.
8 Anna Turja wanted to begin a new life in Finland.
9 The third-class cabins were a long way above the other
   passengers' cabins.
10 There were four beds in every third-class cabin.

Read Chapters 3 and 4. Who said these things?

Thomas Andrews / Mrs Astor / Frederick Fleet / Bruce Ismay / Niels Jensen / First Officer Murdoch / Captain Smith

1 'I know all about this ship.'
2 'We're like a small city, aren't we?'
3 'We don't want to arrive in New York a day early, do we?'
4 'Come on, Captain, let's get there early. The *Titanic* is going to be famous!'
5 'There's an iceberg in front of the ship!'
6 'Stop the engines, quickly!'
7 'Come on, Carla, get up. Something's happening.'

Read Chapters 5 and 6. Match these halves of sentences.

1 The captain got out of bed quickly when . . .
2 When the captain and officers went down into the ship . . .
3 The ship started to sink because . . .
4 The radio operator Jack Phillips . . .
5 The *Californian* stopped that night because . . .
6 The *Californian* didn't get the *Titanic*'s message, because . . .
7 The *Carpathia* came to help the *Titanic*, but . . .
8 People on the *Californian* saw some rockets, but . . .

a they found a lot of holes.
b it was a long way away.
c he heard the noise of the iceberg.
d the radio operator was in bed.
e sent an emergency message.
f they didn't understand them.
g there was water in five compartments.
h the officers knew about the icebergs in the sea.

Before you read Chapter 7, can you guess what happens? Choose Y (yes) or N (no) for each sentence.

1 Everyone on the ship gets into the lifeboats. Y / N
2 The *Titanic* sinks suddenly. Y / N
3 Most of the men stay on the ship. Y / N
4 All the lifeboats are full when they go into the sea. Y / N
5 Mrs Astor says goodbye to her husband. Y / N
6 The third-class passengers stay on E deck. Y / N

Read Chapters 7 and 8. Choose the best question-words for these questions, and then answer them.

How many / What / Why

1 . . . lifeboats did the *Titanic* have?
2 . . . was Mrs Astor cold?
3 . . . did Mrs Straus stay on the ship?
4 . . . did Daniel Buckley put on when he got into a lifeboat?
5 . . . many musicians were there on the ship?
6 . . . kind of music did the musicians play?
7 . . . was it difficult to get into Lifeboat B?
8 . . . people did Harold Lowe take out of the sea alive?
9 . . . could the people in the lifeboats see in the morning?

Read Chapter 9. Put these events in the right order.

1 The *Carpathia* arrived in New York.
2 The *Californian* started to go towards the *Carpathia*.
3 Senator Smith angrily asked Bruce Ismay a lot of questions.
4 The *Carpathia* heard a radio message from the *Titanic*.
5 The *Carpathia* sent some rockets into the air.
6 All the passengers on the lifeboats got onto the *Carpathia*.
7 The *Carpathia* came quickly towards the *Titanic*.

Read Chapter 10. Complete the sentences with the right names.

Mr Astor / Mrs Astor / Daniel Buckley / Millvina Dean / Sidney Goodwin / Colonel Archibald Gracie / Bruce Ismay / Carla Jensen / Second Officer Charles Lightoller / Anna Turja

1 . . . was buried in New York.
2 . . . went back to England with her mother and brother.
3 . . . met her husband in America.
4 . . . had a baby son, and she called him John Jacob.
5 . . . wrote a book about the *Titanic*, but died later that year.
6 . . . was called 'the unknown child' at first, and was buried in Canada.
7 . . . was not happy in his later life.
8 . . . went back to Denmark, and had three children.
9 . . . worked on another ship and that ship sank too.
10 . . . went to France as a soldier, and died four years later.

Read Chapter 11. Answer these questions.

1 What was the name of Walter Lord's book about the *Titanic*?
2 When Anna Turja went to see a film about the *Titanic*, why did she go with her son?
3 How much money did James Cameron need for his film *Titanic*?
4 How much of the film is true?
5 Who was the youngest passenger on the *Titanic*?
6 How old was she when she went across the Atlantic again?
7 What was the name of the ship that took her?

ACTIVITIES

After Reading

1 **Use the clues below to complete this crossword with words from the story. Then find the hidden nine-letter word in the crossword.**

1 Words that one person sends to another.
2 You use this to take photos.
3 A small boat on a ship that people can use if it is not safe on the ship.
4 A long, narrow passage that joins rooms in a building or ship.
5 A machine that makes something move (the *Titanic* had three).
6 Jack Phillips was a radio _____ on the *Titanic*.
7 "The *Titanic* can never _____," said the ship's designer.
8 When the weather is very cold, water becomes _____.
9 Millvina Dean was a nine-week-old _____ when she was a passenger on the *Titanic*.

The hidden word in the crossword is _____.

2 Here are two reports about the *Titanic* from the other ships'
   captains. Use these words to fill in the gaps.

   answer, anything, ask, away, because, bed, find, helped,
   hot, icebergs, lifeboats, light, message, need, passengers,
   rockets, sinking, stopped, tell

REPORT FROM CAPTAIN ROSTRON
OF THE *CARPATHIA*

Our radio operator called the *Titanic* because he had a
_____ for one of the _____. But the radio operator on
the *Titanic* said "We _____ help. We are _____!" So we
began to go towards the *Titanic* at once. We were more
than 90 kilometres _____, and it took us three hours. It
was dangerous because there were a lot of _____, but we
didn't stop. In the end we arrived at the right place, but we
couldn't _____ the *Titanic*. There were just some _____.
The *Titanic* was already under the sea. The passengers
were cold and tired. We _____ them onto the *Carpathia*,
and gave them coats and _____ drinks.

REPORT FROM CAPTAIN LORD
OF THE *CALIFORNIAN*

We _____ at 10.30 that night _____ there was ice in the
sea. We saw a big ship at just after 11 o'clock. I wanted
to _____ them about the ice. We tried to send a message
with a _____, but the other ship didn't _____. We
couldn't hear any messages on the radio because Evans,
our radio operator, was in _____. Soon the other ship
stopped. An hour later, we saw some _____, but we
couldn't understand them. Evans got out of bed at 5.40

in the morning. We saw more rockets then, and Evans called the ship to _____ about them. The ship was the *Carpathia*. They told us about the *Titanic* and the iceberg. Of course, we went towards the *Carpathia* at once. We wanted to help. But the *Titanic* was under the sea. We could not do _____ .

3 **Do you think these people were right or wrong to do these things? Why?**

1 Bruce Ismay asked the captain to get to New York early.
2 The radio operator on the *Carpathia* went to bed at 11.30 p.m.
3 The officers on the *Californian* didn't do anything when they first saw the rockets over the *Titanic*.
4 Mr Straus and his wife stayed on the ship.
5 Daniel Buckley got into a lifeboat with the women.
6 The musicians stayed on the ship.
7 Robert Ballard found the *Titanic* many years later and took lots of photographs.

4 **Find out more about one of the people in the story, and make a poster or give a talk to your class. For example:**

John Jacob Astor	Madeleine Astor
Bruce Ismay	Harold Bride
Charles Lightoller	Captain Lord

You can find more information from these websites:

www.encyclopedia-titanica.org
www.titanic-online.com
http://en.wikipedia.org/wiki/Titanic

ABOUT THE AUTHOR

Tim Vicary was born in London in 1949. He attended Cambridge University and then worked as a schoolteacher, and is now a teaching fellow at the Norwegian Study Centre at the University of York. He is married, has two children and lives in the country in Yorkshire, in the north of England. He has written coursebooks for use in Norwegian secondary schools, and has also published two historical novels, *The Blood Upon the Rose*, and *Cat and Mouse,* under his own name, and a crime novel, *A Game of Proof,* under the pseudonym Megan Stark.

He has written about 20 books for Oxford Bookworms, from Starter to Stage 3. His other Oxford Bookworms titles at Stage 1 are *The Coldest Place on Earth* (True Stories), *The Elephant Man* (True Stories), *Mary, Queen of Scots* (True Stories), *The Murder of Mary Jones* (Playscripts), *Mutiny on the Bounty* (True Stories), *Pocahontas* (True Stories), and *White Death* (Thriller and Adventure).

OXFORD BOOKWORMS LIBRARY

Classics • Crime & Mystery • Factfiles • Fantasy & Horror
Human Interest • Playscripts • Thriller & Adventure
True Stories • World Stories

The OXFORD BOOKWORMS LIBRARY provides enjoyable reading in English, with a wide range of classic and modern fiction, non-fiction, and plays. It includes original and adapted texts in seven carefully graded language stages, which take learners from beginner to advanced level. An overview is given on the next pages.

All Stage 1 titles are available as audio recordings, as well as over eighty other titles from Starter to Stage 6. All Starters and many titles at Stages 1 to 4 are specially recommended for younger learners. Every Bookworm is illustrated, and Starters and Factfiles have full-colour illustrations.

The OXFORD BOOKWORMS LIBRARY also offers extensive support. Each book contains an introduction to the story, notes about the author, a glossary, and activities. Additional resources include tests and worksheets, and answers for these and for the activities in the books. There is advice on running a class library, using audio recordings, and the many ways of using Oxford Bookworms in reading programmes. Resource materials are available on the website <www.oup.com/bookworms>.

The *Oxford Bookworms Collection* is a series for advanced learners. It consists of volumes of short stories by well-known authors, both classic and modern. Texts are not abridged or adapted in any way, but carefully selected to be accessible to the advanced student.

You can find details and a full list of titles in the *Oxford Bookworms Library Catalogue* and *Oxford English Language Teaching Catalogues*, and on the website <www.oup.com/bookworms>.

THE OXFORD BOOKWORMS LIBRARY
GRADING AND SAMPLE EXTRACTS

STARTER • 250 HEADWORDS

present simple – present continuous – imperative –
can/cannot, must – *going to* (future) – simple gerunds ...

Her phone is ringing – but where is it?

Sally gets out of bed and looks in her bag. No phone. She looks under the bed. No phone. Then she looks behind the door. There is her phone. Sally picks up her phone and answers it. *Sally's Phone*

STAGE 1 • 400 HEADWORDS

... past simple – coordination with *and*, *but*, *or* –
subordination with *before*, *after*, *when*, *because*, *so* ...

I knew him in Persia. He was a famous builder and I worked with him there. For a time I was his friend, but not for long. When he came to Paris, I came after him – I wanted to watch him. He was a very clever, very dangerous man. *The Phantom of the Opera*

STAGE 2 • 700 HEADWORDS

... present perfect – *will* (future) – *(don't) have to, must not, could* –
comparison of adjectives – simple *if* clauses – past continuous –
tag questions – *ask/tell* + infinitive ...

While I was writing these words in my diary, I decided what to do. I must try to escape. I shall try to get down the wall outside. The window is high above the ground, but I have to try. I shall take some of the gold with me – if I escape, perhaps it will be helpful later. *Dracula*

STAGE 3 • 1000 HEADWORDS

... should, may – present perfect continuous – *used to* – past perfect –
causative – relative clauses – indirect statements ...

Of course, it was most important that no one should see
Colin, Mary, or Dickon entering the secret garden. So Colin
gave orders to the gardeners that they must all keep away
from that part of the garden in future. *The Secret Garden*

STAGE 4 • 1400 HEADWORDS

... past perfect continuous – passive (simple forms) –
would conditional clauses – indirect questions –
relatives with *where/when* – gerunds after prepositions/phrases ...

I was glad. Now Hyde could not show his face to the world
again. If he did, every honest man in London would be proud
to report him to the police. *Dr Jekyll and Mr Hyde*

STAGE 5 • 1800 HEADWORDS

... future continuous – future perfect –
passive (modals, continuous forms) –
would have conditional clauses – modals + perfect infinitive ...

If he had spoken Estella's name, I would have hit him. I was so
angry with him, and so depressed about my future, that I could
not eat the breakfast. Instead I went straight to the old house.
Great Expectations

STAGE 6 • 2500 HEADWORDS

... passive (infinitives, gerunds) – advanced modal meanings –
clauses of concession, condition

When I stepped up to the piano, I was confident. It was as if I
knew that the prodigy side of me really did exist. And when I
started to play, I was so caught up in how lovely I looked that
I didn't worry how I would sound. *The Joy Luck Club*

BOOKWORMS · TRUE STORIES · STAGE 1

The Coldest Place on Earth

TIM VICARY

In the summer of 1910, a race began. A race to be the first man at the South Pole, in Antarctica. Robert Falcon Scott, an Englishman, left London in his ship, the Terra Nova, and began the long journey south. Five days later, another ship also began to travel south. And on this ship was Roald Amundsen, a Norwegian.

But Antarctica is the coldest place on earth, and it is a long, hard journey over the ice to the South Pole. Some of the travellers never returned to their homes again.

This is the story of Scott and Amundsen, and of one of the most famous and dangerous races in history.

BOOKWORMS · FACTFILES · STAGE 2

Ireland

TIM VICARY

There are many different Irelands. There is the Ireland of peaceful rivers, green fields, and beautiful islands. There is the Ireland of song and dance, pubs and theatres – the country of James Joyce, Bob Geldof, and Riverdance. And there is the Ireland of guns, fighting, death, and the hope of peace. Come with us and visit all of these Irelands – and many more . . .